Sticker Spelling for School

Written by Susan Barraclough
Illustrated by Ian Cunliffe

Ladybird

A to Z

There are 26 letters in the alphabet. Add stickers to make the alphabet complete.

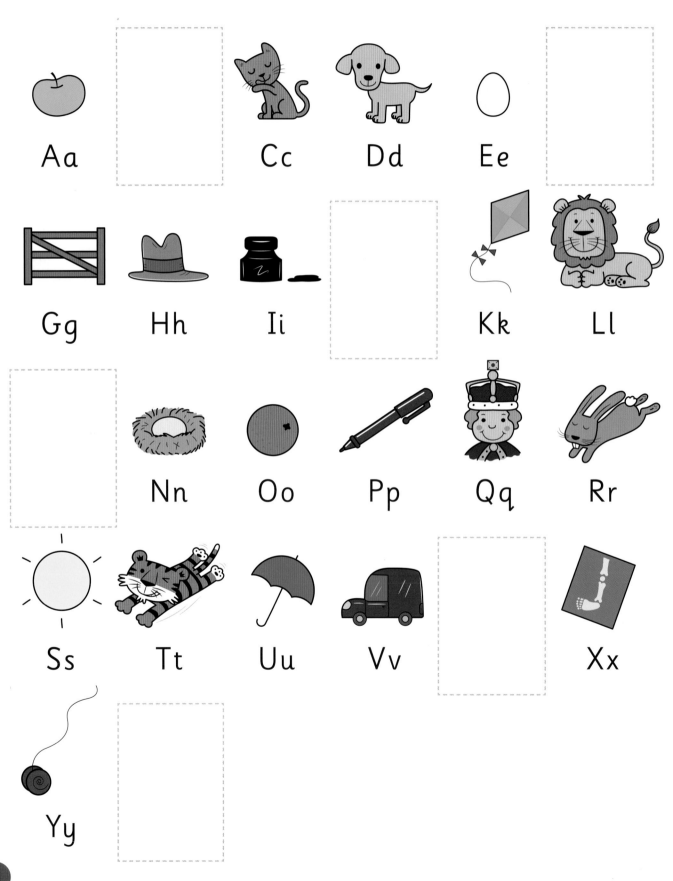

Aa Cc Dd Ee

Gg Hh Ii Kk Ll

Nn Oo Pp Qq Rr

Ss Tt Uu Vv Xx

Yy

Look at the pictures in column 1. Can you see two things that begin with the same letter sound? Find a sticker which makes the same letter sound and place it at the bottom of column 1. Then do the same for the next columns. What do the letters spell?

1	2	3	4	5

A to Z – Vowels

Five letters of the alphabet are called **vowels**. The other 21 are called **consonants**.

a   **e**   **i**   **o**   **u**

Write **a** or **e** to complete these words.

c_t   h_n   t_p   b_d

Write **i** or **o** to complete these words.

d_g   p_n   p_g   f_x

Write **u** or **e** to complete these words.

s_n   p_g   j_g   p_n

These words all have **short** vowel sounds.

Sometimes vowels have a different sound. These words have **long** vowel sounds.

Write **a**, **e**, **i**, **o** or **u** to complete these words.

c _ k e   b _ e   k _ t e

n _ t e   fl _ t e

Add a picture sticker for each word. Say the words and listen for the vowel sounds. Draw a line to match the words that rhyme.

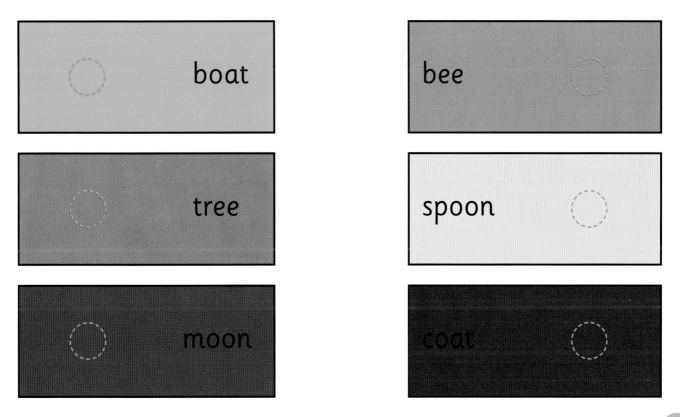

boat   bee

tree   spoon

moon   coat

Plurals – adding s and es

We usually make nouns, or naming words, **plural** by **adding the letter s** to the end of the word. Add a sticker to make each word mean more than one.

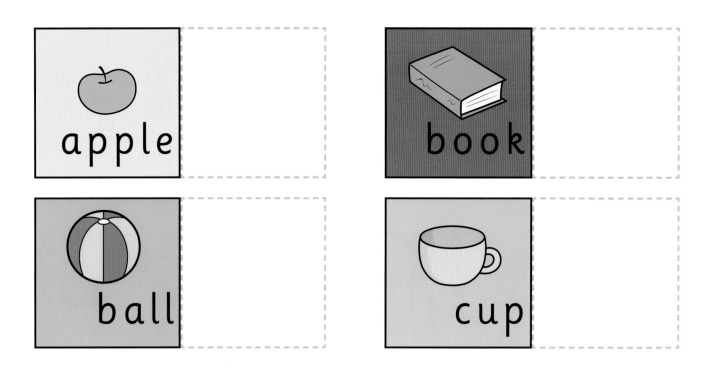

When a noun ends in the letters **s**, **x**, **sh** or **ch** we usually make it plural by **adding the letters es** to the end of the word. Add a sticker to make each word mean more than one.

Plurals – adding ies and irregular plurals

When a noun ends in a **consonant** followed by the letter **y**, such as **baby**, we **take off the y and add the letters ies** to the end of the word.
Add a picture for each of these words.

one baby   two babies   one lorry   two lorries

one puppy   three puppies   one fairy   four fairies

Some words do not follow a rule when there is more than one thing.
Can you add a word sticker to fill in the missing words?

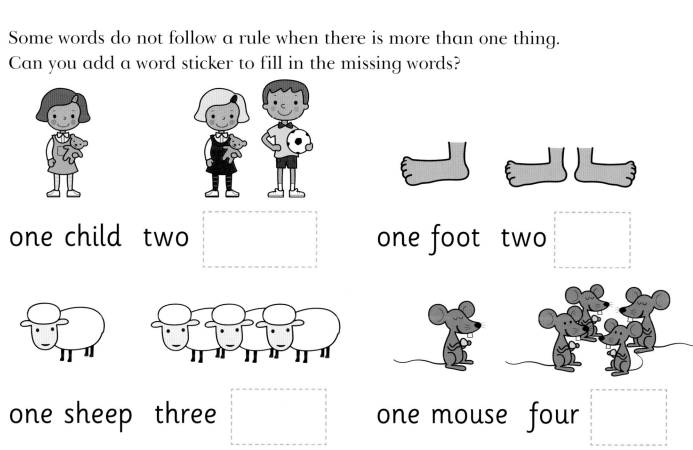

one child   two   one foot   two

one sheep   three   one mouse   four

Making an adjective by adding y

Adjectives are describing words, such as **big** and **friendly**. Some adjectives can be made by **adding y** to a noun. Look at the pictures below, and add a word sticker to describe each picture.

The words below have short vowel sounds. To make these words into adjectives you must **double the last letter and then add y**. Look at the first example and then change the other words to adjectives. Find a picture sticker for each word.

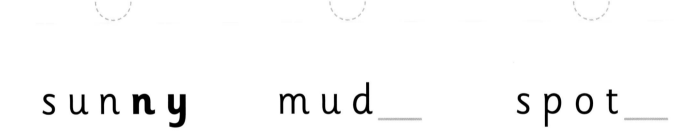

sun**n y**   mud_   spot_

If a noun ends with **e, take off the e and add y** to make an adjective. Write the adjectives. The first one has been done for you.

wave   wavy   rose   _____

stone _____   nose _____

slime _____   ice _____

Fill in the weather chart with the missing weather word stickers.

Monday		
Tuesday		
Wednesday		
Thursday		
Friday		
Saturday		
Sunday		

Was it sunny or rainy on Monday? _____

Was it windy or snowy on Thursday? _____

Was it windy or cloudy on Wednesday? _____

Was it sunny or stormy on Friday? _____

Was it rainy or windy on Tuesday? _____

Making comparisons by adding er and est

We can **add er or est** to the end of many adjectives to compare them.
Add the missing picture stickers and finish spelling the words below.

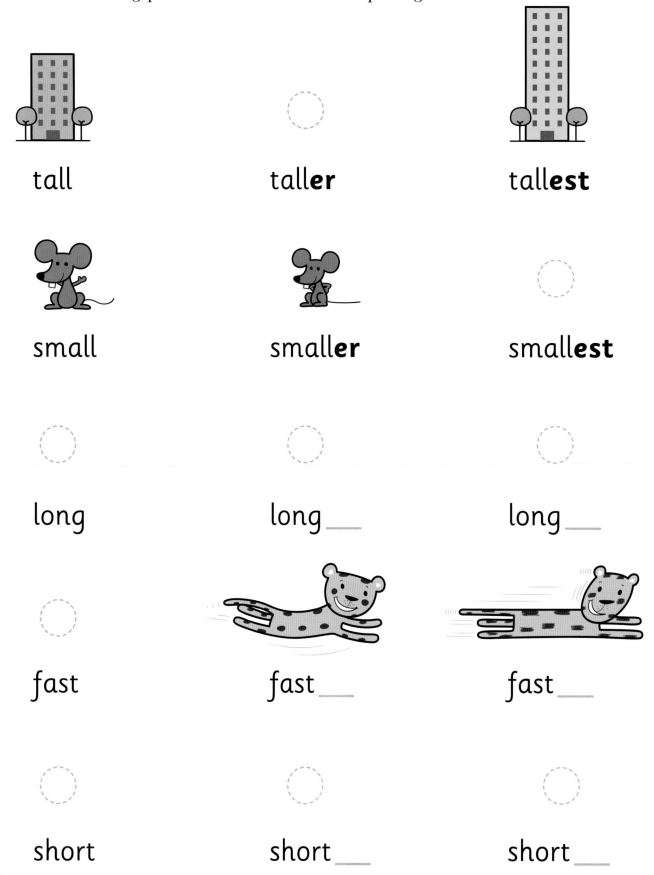

tall

taller

tallest

small

smaller

smallest

long

long___

long___

fast

fast___

fast___

short

short___

short___

If the adjective ends in the letter **y, change the y to an i before adding er or est**. The first clown is **funny**, the second clown is **funnier** and the third clown is **funniest**. Can you label the dirty boys with word stickers in the same way?

funny

funn**ier**

funn**iest**

Look at the animals in each box, then circle the **smallest** butterfly, the **biggest** elephant, the **hairiest** bear and the **stripiest** tiger.

smallest

biggest

hairiest

stripiest

Changing verbs by adding ing

We **add ing** to the end of many **verbs**, or doing words, to show that something is happening now. Add a word sticker to describe what each child is doing.

When a word has a **short** vowel sound (such as the sound **o** in **hop**) we **double the last letter before** we **add ing**. Spell the 'ing' words below.

hopping

sit ___

dig ___

When the word ends in **e**, we **take off the e** before we **add ing**. Write the new words here. The first one has been done for you.

ride + ing = riding   make + ing = _____

care + ing = _____   smile + ing = _____

move + ing = _____   hope + ing = _____

A to Z – page 2

| Ww | Ff | Zz | Mm | Bb | Jj |

A to Z – page 3

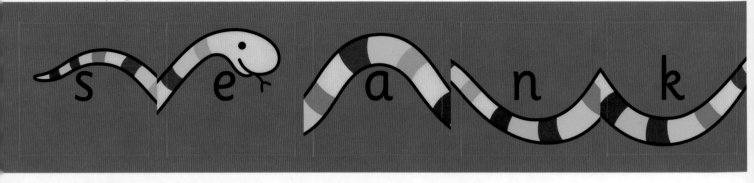

s   e   a   n   k

A to Z – Vowels page 5

Plurals – adding s and es page 6

Changing verbs by adding ed – pages 14 and 15

pulled   pushed

	gave	wrote	slept
rang	ran	sang	sat	stood	blew

Adding un and other word beginnings – page 16

untie

untidy

Homophones – page 18

sun   blew   flour   leek

Homonyms – pages 20 and 21

lamb   knife   wreck   yolk   gnome   whale

Compound words – page 22

snowman   rainbow   lighthouse   wallpaper

Compound words – page 23

horse star bag flower sea sun

fish hand

Reward chart – page 24

Plurals – adding ies and irregular plurals page 7

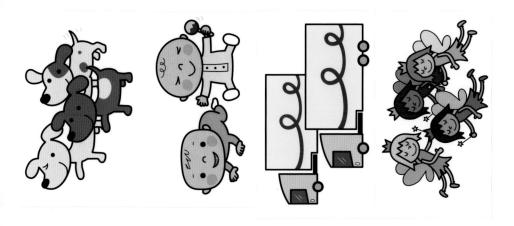

children sheep

feet mice

Making an adjective by adding y – pages 8 and 9

hair**y** smell**y** dir**ty**

 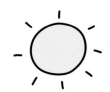 

stormy

rainy icy cloudy

snowy sunny windy

Making comparisons by adding er and est – pages 10 and 11

 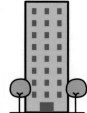 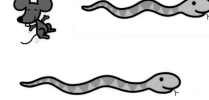 

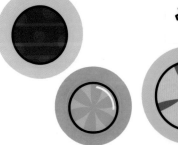

dirt**iest** dirt**ier** dirty

Changing verbs by adding ing – pages 12 and 13

playing walking looking jumping reading kicking

There is a ball missing from each picture. Add a ball sticker to each one, then write the missing action word.

The girl is
_____ a ball.

The baby is
_____ a ball.

The boy is
_____ a ball.

The clown is
_____ 3 balls.

Changing verbs by adding ed

We **add ed** to the end of many verbs to show that something has already happened. Read each word, then find a sticker that spells the word in the past tense.

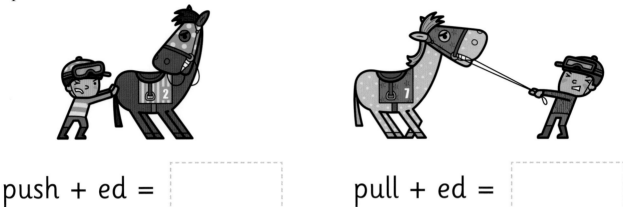

push + ed = [ ]   pull + ed = [ ]

When the word contains a **short** vowel sound (such as the sound **u** in **rub**) we **double the last letter and then add ed**. Complete each of these verbs with the correct spelling.

c l a p ___   j o g ___   h o p ___

When the word ends in **e, take off the e and add ed**. Write each verb with the correct spelling. The first one is done for you.

like + ed = liked   race + ed = _____

smile + ed = _____   hope + ed = _____

wave + ed = _____   save + ed = _____

The verbs below are **irregular verbs**. They do not end in **ed** when we talk about things that have already happened. Look at each verb and picture, then add the missing stickers.

eat ate

run

sit

blow

sing

ring

write

give

stand

sleep

Adding un and other word beginnings

We can **add un** to the beginning of some words to make them mean the opposite. Read each word and then find a picture or word sticker to show the opposite.

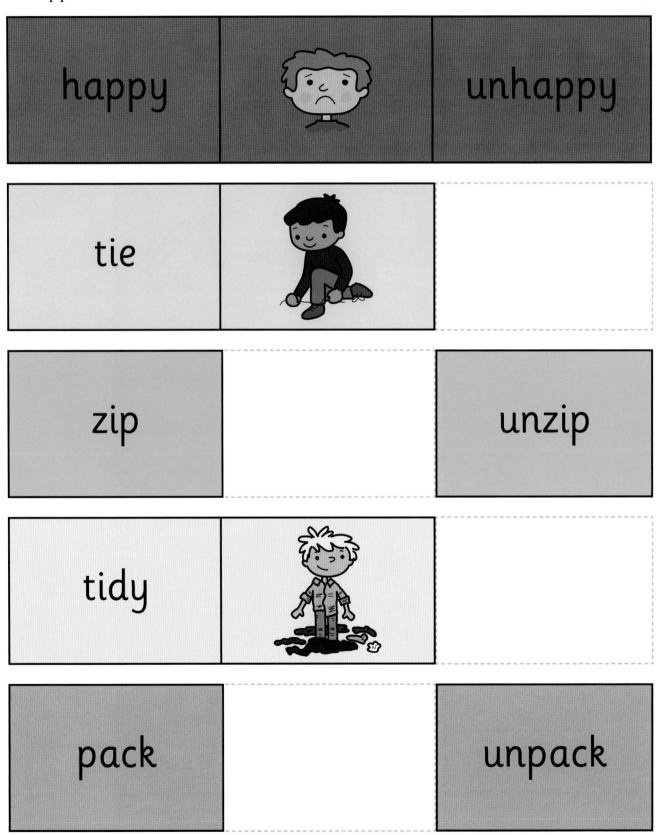

happy		unhappy
tie		
zip		unzip
tidy		
pack		unpack

Suffixes: ful, ly, less

This story has some word endings missing. Add one of these endings in the spaces below:

ful   ly   less

Wendy and her mummy and daddy had just moved house. Mummy said, "You've been very help____, Wendy. I think you deserve a treat."
She took out a big box.
In the box, curled up quiet____, was a hamster.

"He's yours, Wendy, and he's very friend____ and play____."

At first Wendy was afraid but slow____ she felt braver. "Don't worry, he's quite harm____," said Wendy's mummy.

Wendy bought the hamster a colour____ red and orange cage with a wheel. She looked after him always, never forgot his food and was never care____ when she held him. Wendy and her hamster were soon the best of friends.

Homophones

Homophones are words that sound the same but have a different spelling and meaning. Add the picture stickers to sort the homophones into pairs.

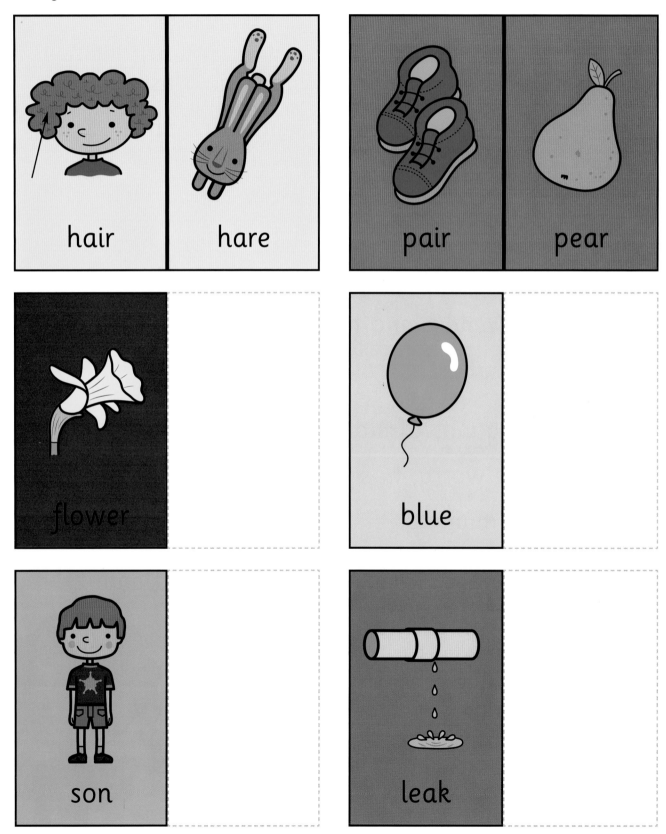

hair

hare

pair

pear

flower

blue

son

leak

Look at the homophones at the top of each box. Read the words then write them in the sentence.

blew   blue

She _____ up the _____ balloon.

sea   see

He can _____ the _____.

I   eye

_____ have a sore _____.

write   right

Did you _____ the _____ answer?

Homonyms

Homonyms are words that sound the same and are spelt the same, but have different meanings. Each of these words has two meanings. Can you add another picture sticker for each word?

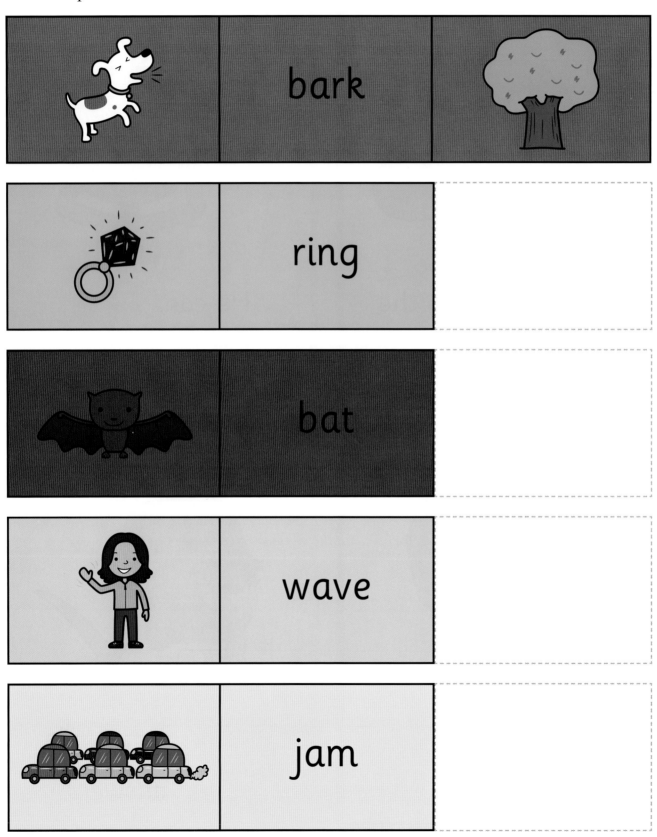

These words should all have silent letters in them. Say the name for each object and find the sticker with the correct spelling of each word.

Here are some more words with silent letters. Can you add a picture sticker for each word?

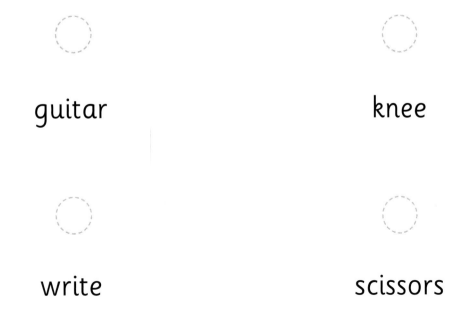

guitar

knee

write

scissors

Compound words

Can you add a picture sticker to answer each of these word sums?

foot + ball = football

snow + man =

wall + paper =

rain + bow =

light + house =

Read the words in the word sum and then write the answer.

some + thing = _____   every + one = _____

any + thing = _____   some + one = _____

every + thing = _____   hair + brush = _____

Look at the first picture and say its name. Match up two word stickers to make a label for the picture. Then label the other pictures in the same way.

Reward chart

Use this chart to keep a record of your progress. Each time you finish an activity, reward yourself with a star. How many can you collect?

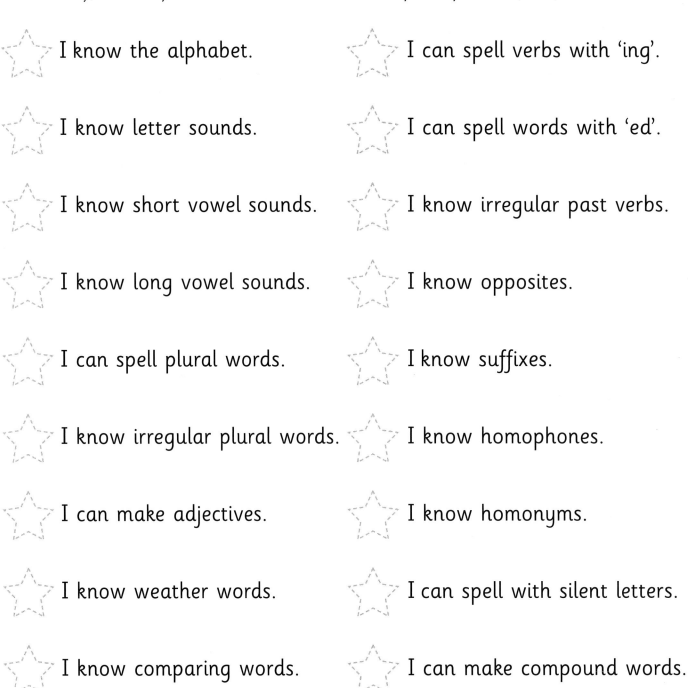

I know the alphabet.

I can spell verbs with 'ing'.

I know letter sounds.

I can spell words with 'ed'.

I know short vowel sounds.

I know irregular past verbs.

I know long vowel sounds.

I know opposites.

I can spell plural words.

I know suffixes.

I know irregular plural words.

I know homophones.

I can make adjectives.

I know homonyms.

I know weather words.

I can spell with silent letters.

I know comparing words.

I can make compound words.

I can spell verbs.

I am really good at spelling!

Congratulations! You have completed the whole book!

24